# Amazon Mom: Rinse and Repeat
## How to Take Your Amazon Business to the Next Level

By Stacy McCafferty

All Rights Reserved. No part of this publication may be reproduced in any form or by any means, including scanning, photocopying, or otherwise without prior written permission of the copyright holder. Copyright © 2014 Stacy McCafferty

This book is dedicated to my parents, Rocky and Ann.

Mom, from a young age you taught me the art of being thrifty and the importance of family above all else. The strong woman you are has helped shape me into the strong woman I am today.

Dad, you have always believed in me even when I didn't believe in myself. And you always knew I would write a book one day – this one's for you!

To the two best parents a girl could ask for…. thank you for everything. I love you both!

# Table of Contents

**Introduction - Who Am I?**
    Who are you?
    Taking the next step
**Part 1: Retail Arbitrage**
**What is retail arbitrage?**
**Where to look**
    Clearance Racks
    Local Stores
    Online Arbitrage
    Discount Stores
    Your Own Home
**How to find winning products**
    In the field
    Google and Store Websites
    Amazon
**Getting creative**
    Multipacks
    Bundles
    Gift Baskets
**My own story**
**Part 2: Wholesale**
**What is Wholesale?**
**First things first**
    Wholesale purchase requirements
**Finding items to wholesale**
    Your own inventory
    Friends
    Google
    Personal Use
**Taking the next step**
**Putting it all together**

# Introduction - Who Am I?

My name is Stacy McCafferty and I'm just your average girl. I am a mortgage underwriter, turned stay at home Mom to three, turned online entrepreneur. I tried everything to earn money at home after my first child was born and I resigned my underwriting position. I had some moderate success in a couple of endeavors but with most I quickly realized what you have probably found yourself ... making a buck while being home with your kids is hard. Darn hard!

Or is it? In my first book, Amazon Mom: One Woman's Journey from Mom to Successful Online Entrepreneur, I went into detail about my many rocky starts and stops at work from home employment up through my eventual happening upon Amazon. I wrote the first Amazon Mom book hoping that my story would inspire others who had been in my shoes. I knew there had to be others of us out there but I was blown away by how many of us there truly are!

In my second book, Amazon Mom: Getting Thrifty with It. How to turn thrift store finds into full time income, I explained how I use thrift store finds to help stock my Amazon inventory, where to look, and what to look for. I'll went into detail on the items I search for and successfully sell the most reliably so you knew what to look for too. I even took you with me on a sample thrift store trip so you can see my personal methods first hand.

In this book, we take the next step beyond thrifting and towards growing a well rounded Amazon business that can weather all seasons and grow as much and as quickly as you are ready for.

## Who are you?
Now that you know a little about me let's talk about you. Who exactly are you?

Maybe you read my first books and have delved into thrifting? Maybe you are enjoying it but can see the limitations and want to take the next step? If so, I can help you!

Maybe you are interested in an Amazon business but have no interest at all in thrifting? It's ok, I'm not offended. That sort of business model is definitely not everyone's cup of tea. But, the good news is that there is more than one way to launch and Amazon business and ... I can help you!

## Taking the next step
I find thrifting to be fabulous and it is something I will always do, both personally and as an important part of my Amazon business. But, the truth is that you won't get rich selling "one of" items. To start generating steady, reliable income you need a sustainable business model. One that allows you to sell and then replenish that inventory with more of the exact same item – something which thrifting most definitely does not do. For that you need to enter the world of retail arbitrage and wholesale selling.

I will be honest, when I first was first starting out and heard these terms bandied about by sellers more experienced than myself... they scared me to death. Just the name retail arbitrage sounds intimidating and I (wrongly) assumed that only big players could sell wholesale and not a small little company like mine.

While common, those feelings couldn't be further from the truth. In the coming chapters I will walk you through both retail arbitrage and wholesale selling and explain why you need to explore both of them for your own business.

The first part of this book will be devoted to the in's and out's of retail arbitrage. How do you find things to sell, where to source items, techniques to help you while out in the field, and my personal experiences out in the trenches.

In the second part of the book we will take things up another notch and look at the world of wholesale selling. I will walk you through what you need to start, how to find items, how to reach out to companies, and share more of my own personal experiences.

So, without further ado … let's get started!

# Part 1:
# Retail Arbitrage

# What is retail arbitrage?

Retail arbitrage (RA), simply put, is when you buy items at retail value and resell them for a profit. These can be items you source at your local store, clearance items, online items, etc. and in the majority of cases they are something you and can replenish at that price over and over again.

After thrifting I don't think there is a better way to get your feet wet and launch an Amazon business. The upfront costs are higher (which is why I still recommend thrifting for those just starting out and motivated to go that route) but if you are careful with your selections you can minimize your risk and see some nice profits. And even better, you can see these profits over and over again.

So, now you know what the heck RA is let's talk about the various ways you can incorporate it into your own business.

Before I tell you what to do I'm going to save you some time and money and tell you what not to do. Don't pay for BOLO's. These are what those in the business call Be On The Lookout For items. On the surface it sounds great… someone does the research and gathers a list of items that can be found at national retailers (either online or in store) and shares that valuable info with you. But, as you probably already know nothing in life is free. These lists almost never are. And even if they were do you want to be given information that is also being given to other Amazon Sellers? I know I don't. I'd rather do the legwork and find my own winning products than come into the game already facing competition.

Ok, great then it's best to find these items on my own. How the heck do I do that?

I won't lie and say that it's easy but nothing worthwhile ever is. The good news is that it's not impossible either. There are endless possibilities and they are all out there waiting for you to find them. Let's talk about the best ways to do that….

# Where to look

Thrifting was easy ... if you want to source inventory you head to thrift stores. But, where do you look to build inventory you can replenish? These are some of my tried and true places:

## Clearance Racks

Every store from time to time needs to move out old merchandise to make room for the new. If you take the time to check out the selection when you are out shopping you can often pick up some nice deals and flip them on Amazon for a profit.

This is actually where I first ventured into the RA game in my own business. It was 4th quarter my first year in business and although I was enjoying the success I was finding with my thrifted items I was starting to hunger for more. And because I was hanging around the online groups and reading everything I could get my hands on I kept seeing retail arbitrage mentioned over and over. It was an interesting next step for my business but I was really new to Amazon and a little intimidated. At that time I was still merchant fulfilling my orders and space was already getting cramped in my basement office. I knew I could make the leap to FBA but was I ready for that? I wasn't sure yet.

My other concern was money. I was still testing my business and up to that point I had been mostly buying and flipping thrift store books although I had very newly started to test the water in the toys category thanks to the Target items now showing up at the Goodwill. It's one thing to put out .97 cents on an item and hope it sold and quite another to put out $5, $10, $15, or more for an item – especially considering besides my fledgling Amazon store we were a one income family who had just bought a house recently and were adjusting to that new expense. I didn't have a ton of capital to play with. But, I knew I needed to step things up, so I could make more money, so I could buy more inventory, so I could make more money ... and so on.

One afternoon I was shopping at our local Walmart for non-Amazon related purchases. Just your regular household shopping trip. I had a little bit of time to kill before I needed to pick up the kids and thought I would take a walk down to the garden department. But, when I got there instead of garden supplies the aisles were FILLED with clearance toys. I grabbed my phone and started to scan. Bingo!! I found a few items that were low rank and in some cases had many units available for only a few dollars. I took a deep breath, loaded up the cart, and hit the register.

That trip, in addition to the recent Target items I was seeing at the Goodwill's, made quite a pile in my basement office and led me to make the leap to FBA. No way could I keep up with all of those orders and as I would find out moving my inventory to FBA not only freed up space it also increased my sales as well as the profit I could make on each item.

## Local Stores

Clearance is great but I'll be honest ... I hesitated to consider it retail arbitrage. What gave me pause is that you can't always replenish the items. Or if you can it may be at full price and not at a price where you can make a profit on Amazon. In the end I decided that it does belong under the arbitrage umbrella because it isn't thrift store sourcing and is done at traditional retail outlets.

But, as you add retail arbitrage to your arsenal you will want to find products that you can not only flip for a profit but products you can flip for a profit over and over and over again. Buy, sell, buy, sell …rinse and repeat.

A great place to find these items are the stores right in your town. Those stores that you stop at for your own personal shopping needs have aisles and aisle filled with things that you can sell on Amazon, you just have to find them!

When I was really focusing on RA I would take a few minutes every time I was in a store and pick an area of the store to source. I didn't always find a lot of new items to sell but often I would find at least one or two.

## Online Arbitrage

With three kids that always seem to be moving in different directions I don't always have the time to spend at the physical stores trying to find those needle in the haystacks. Enter online sourcing.

Whenever you have a few minutes you can get online and start looking for deals. Check the online sites of the stores you already shop. What I like to do is open Amazon on one tab and the sites on another so I can easily see what the demand is for items and what the going prices are as I source them.

You can even use Amazon to find products. If you go under the category you are interested in selling in you can find all kinds of useful information and lists to see what is selling the most and for the highest prices and then look for similar items to offer that may not be on Amazon yet or if they are don't have a lot of competition.

## Discount Stores

These stores can be a real boon to your business. Dollar stores, 5 Below, Big Lots, and similar type stores offer prices that fit most business models and you can often find items there that are selling for much more on Amazon.

Another great place to look is discount grocery stores. These stores buy out lots from other stores or companies for a fraction of the cost often because of the expiration dates but sometimes simply because the item is being discontinued or the packaging has changed (this is very common when the packaging has a seasonal theme of some kind).

FBA requires expiration dates to be 90 days out so that will greatly limit what you can find but don't give up hope. Don't give up hope though … all you need to do if find a discontinued product or two that has a large following (and a far out expiration date) and you will be very happy you made the stop. I've come across many of this type of product over the past two years and they are always very, very profitable.

## Your Own Home

Sometimes inspiration can be found in your own pantry. Companies are constantly coming out with new sizes, flavors, items and these aren't always on Amazon yet. If something looks interesting that I have picked up for my own family I'll often give it a quick scan as I'm putting away groceries and see if it's something I need to look into for Amazon too.

I've even been known from time to time to give my whole pantry a scan. It doesn't take terribly long, is done from the comfort of my own home, and can turn up some surprising finds.

# How to find winning products

Now that you know where to look the next step is knowing how to find items that are worth adding to your inventory.

I have three main techniques I use when sourcing new items.

## In the field

This is the sourcing I do when I'm at the local stores. The idea is an easy one ... find products and sell them. But, the implementation when faced with SO MANY aisles of options can be downright overwhelming. So what do I do? I pick a general category that I'm interested in or that I think will sell well on Amazon and every time I'm in a store I take a shelf or two and scan everything.

EVERYTHING. While I trust my instincts when thrifting this is an area where I need to rely on scanning and I do. As I find items that are promising I will text myself the name of the product and cost to buy so I can do some more research at home and don't waste too much precious in store time.

Insider tip: If you are short on time or if you are shy of scanning items out in the open like that you can always use your phone to snap a quick picture of a shelf and then look up the items later when you have time and privacy.

Once home I go through my list of potential winners and pull the items up on Amazon to verify that it is indeed an item I want to sell. If it is my next question is how I want to sell it. Some items I will sell FBA if the cost to buy them isn't more than I care to spend AND if the rank is low enough that I feel confident that the cost will be returned quickly so I can buy more product.

If the ROI is high but so is the purchase cost oftentimes I will add it to my inventory but do it as a Merchant Fulfilled item. The beauty of selling a percentage of my inventory this way is that I am not out the cost until I get an order. And if it never sells at my price, no harm no foul.

## Google and Store Websites

Google can be an incredibly useful tool for finding items to sell. Some afternoons I'll spend an hour or so while watching a movie with the kids and just look for inspiration. I will google things like "hot products", "best (insert category) of the year", "best (insert category) you have never heard of", etc. As lists pop up I cross reference them with Amazon and hope to find some new leads. I've found a lot of new products this way.

Store websites can work in a similar way and I've used this to my advantage plenty of times. Most of the big box stores (Walmart, Target, and the like) have the ability to sort categories by Top 100, Bestsellers, ect. This info is invaluable and can give you a great place find items that aren't on Amazon yet.

## Amazon

Believe it or not, Amazon itself can give you some great ideas. I typically use Amazon searches to identify items that either are not sold FBA and could be or items that are not sold FBA because they can't be (due to expiration dates or packaging) but that I could offer for a lower price than the competition is.

I find this especially helpful in my grocery lines that I fill myself. I've found a lot of what I currently sell via these searches. Either it will identify brands that sell very well and for a high ROI and I will expand Amazon's offerings and add more from the line to my own inventory or the items are being sold at such inflated prices that I can come in much lower and get the sale. And because these items are Merchant Fulfilled and I am not spending a penny unless an order comes in I can ensure I won't get into a price war with another seller. If that starts to happen I simply drop out and don't sell that item anymore.

# Getting creative

Just because an item is already on Amazon and the competition is stiff all is not always lost. There are things you can do to still include this item in your own inventory … you just need to get creative!

## Multipacks

A multipack is when you sell an item in a pack of more than one. Some buyers would rather order several of an item than just one and this can give you a leg up on your competition. And it can save you some time while listing and produce more return from each sale. Win-win!

## Bundles

A bundle is when you sell related items together for one price under one listing. You can get really creative with these but remember that to list as a bundle on Amazon your bundle must make sense and the items must really be related to each other.

You might consider selling a bundle that includes a personal recipe and the ingredients needed to make it. Or items to make a popular craft. The more creative you are the better your chance to be unique and hopefully get the sale.

## Gift Baskets

These are hugely popular and the themes you can come up with are endless. Since they can get pricey I would probably sell them merchant fulfilled so you can buy supplies and send them out as you get orders.

# My own story

Now that we have gone over exactly what retail arbitrage is, why you should consider it for your own business, and how to go about it maybe you are wondering where it fits into my own business.

I will be honest with you and tell you that while RA was the second important step I took in growing my business to where it is today it is also a very small part of my current business model. It was something I need to learn and something I'm glad I did but I enjoy thrifting so much more. Paying those discounted prices has really spoiled me and it's just plain fun!

But, there is one area where RA is still very much a part of my business and that is in local, merchant fulfilled grocery items. These are items that I can source locally but are not available to the national market. And because I favor MF over FBA for most of my retail arbitrage items these are also items that can't be sold via FBA. I have no interest in competing on an FBA listing as an MF seller… I'll never win the sale.

Instead, I source local items that are perishable to some degree. Often they are shelf stable but have short expiration date that excludes them from FBA. The local aspect of these items already limits my competition and in most cases I don't have any. Because of this and because of the demand in other parts of the country for items that are not available there I can command high prices for fairly inexpensive items. And I always set my shipping to at least cover the flat rate option that will fit the order so even if the order goes across the country I will be covered and able to offer two day priority shipping.

There are one or two items that I do sell FBA. These are items that started as items I filled myself but because they did qualify for FBA and because there was little or no competition and orders were pretty steady I moved them over to FBA and keep a stock of 3 or 4 at all times. I replenish them as they sell, usually about once a month, and keep on rinsing and repeating.

So, that is the glamourous world of retail arbitrage. What's next, you ask? The wonderful world of wholesale! Come on, follow me….

# Part 2:
# Wholesale

# What is Wholesale?

Wholesale is when you buy items at a discounted price not available to the general public (wholesale pricing is only available to resellers) directly from a company and resell it for a profit.

Wholesale appeals both to my need to buy things at a discount (I'm nothing if not thrifty) and my desire to build and inventory that I can easily replenish as I sell. And because wholesale orders are generally placed online or over the phone and shipped to you there isn't much out there that is easier or more profitable for your business. It definitely takes rinse and repeat to a higher level.

But, for some reason it's scary. Darn scary. Or at least it was for me and it was for that reason that I dragged my feet far longer than I should have before testing the waters and really taking my business to the next level.

I had already been selling on Amazon for over a year and a half, had mastered thrifting, and had explored retail arbitrage enough to know what fit into my business and what didn't. I had even taken the steps to make my business "legit" and had named my company, registered with my state, and gotten my resellers cert. My little company, born from selling my husband's textbooks, was earning me real income and was a true business. So, why was I afraid to take that next step and start to wholesale?

Up until this point I had been operating largely under the radar. Even with the paperwork filed I was still thinking of my business as a "hobby" and not something with which the sky is the limit. In my mind I was a Mom with a side job and not a Business owner who could interact with other companies in that space.

But, the truth is that I was ready. I just needed belief in myself and a nudge in the right direction. That nudge came because of thrifting. About 6 months prior I had come across a large amount of a specialty soap at the Goodwill. It was a natural company (along the line of Burt's Bees) and the product was an organic soap that keeps away mosquitoes. At the time all I cared about was the fact that Goodwill was selling them in bags of about 8 bars for about $4 and they were selling on Amazon for $15 each merchant fulfilled. And there were many bags of them available… I took them all. I listed them for $25 each because I was selling them FBA and off they went.

And there they sat. It was after all winter and not really mosquito season for most of the country. Honestly, I forgot about them until the weather warmed and, low and behold, orders started to pour in. I was getting the $25 a bar and they were moving fast. The product had fantastic reviews and, even though I had never heard of it, it was obvious some people had!

I quickly sold through my stock and I was wondering where I could get more. I had no idea what the product even retailed for (although I was sure it wasn't $25) and I set out with an idea to turn it a retail arbitrage item in my inventory.

I found the website and saw that it was retailing for $9 (Yes, really. I told you people will pay more for the convenience of Amazon!). That was a good start and I considered placing an order but before I did something caught my eye: A wholesale option. They had a whole portal you could access and order from if you provided your reseller info and were approved. It was all done on line, which took out some of the intimidation factor for me and I applied. Once I was accepted I saw that

I could buy the same item wholesale for $4 each. WOW!!! They did have an initial order requirement (more on this in a bit as most companies do) so I selected several items, took a deep breath, and entered the world of wholesaling.

The items arrived shortly thereafter and I can't tell you how much easier the prep (there was none) and listing was than what I was used to. I had it ready to go to Amazon in about 10 minutes and once there they continued to sell steadily and I placed a couple more orders over the summer.

And with that one order I was hooked. You see, my three kids were now out of school for three long months and if you have ever sourced thrift stores with kids in tow (especially multiple kids) you will understand why I was starting to think of other ways to build my inventory.

Wholesaling was the answer I was looking for. And, if you have been selling on Amazon for long enough to have learned the ropes AND have set your business up with your state, it may be the answer for you too.

# First things first

The Basics
Not just anyone can place a wholesale order.  There are certain basic requirements you will need to have in place before you contact companies and start placing orders:

A Federal Employer Identification Number - You can apply for this right with the IRS on their website and the process usually takes about two weeks.  This is good to have for anyone doing business because it saves you from having to give your personal social security number out and you should do this as soon as you can, but definitely before starting to wholesale.

A resellers certificate from your state –   The name for this actually varies by state (where I live in PA it is a resellers cert) and some states call it a wholesale license, a sellers permit, or a resale permit license.  The permit legally allows you to buy items wholesale and resell them at retail prices and it allows you to not pay sales tax on those purchases.  This is a handy thing to have as you can also present it when making purchases for resale at the thrift stores and your local retail stores and avoid the sales tax on those purchases too.

A Sales tax license and state ID number - You will also need to apply for a sales tax license from the Department of Revenue or the appropriate authority in your state.  At the same time you must apply for a state tax ID number, which allows you to charge taxes to your retail buyers, pay your state taxes and pay your employees.  The procedure and fees on these vary based on your state.

Once you have these in place you are ready to start contacting companies and setting up some wholesale contracts.

## Wholesale purchase requirements

Just as the government has certain requirements in place that must be met before you can start wholesale purchasing, the individual companies often have their own requirements that must be met by those that purchase from them.

In my experience most companies have a higher initial order requirement designed to ensure you are a serious customer and subsequent orders have to meet a lower requirement. In some cases these are dollar amount requirements and in other cases these are requirements for a set number of cases.

Whether you are just starting out or are old hat at selling wholesale I recommend sticking to companies that have lower requirements.  Amazon is an ever changing marketplace and you don't want to be stuck with merchandise you can't move or have to take a loss on because either there is no interest or there is sudden competition.

For example, there was one company that I looked into early on and had to pass on.  They had a product that I had been selling through retail arbitrage (purchased at my local Walmart and sent in via FBA).  I was selling them fairly steadily but the stock at the Walmart was somewhat limited.  Between that and wanting to get a better price and increase my margin on the sales I contacted the company about purchasing wholesale.  I was discouraged, to say the least, when they came back with a wholesale price sheet that noted a whopping 250 case initial order.  Yikes!!  Way too rich for my blood and way too risky for Amazon.  I passed on the opportunity and actually don't even carry the item in my inventory at all at the present time.

What I prefer to do is to identify an product (or two) in a company's line that either I know to sell well because I have sold it before via RA or even thrifting and then look for a low opening order. I prefer around $100 as my risk limit but I will go up to $200-$300 if it is a product I really believe in or if there are multiple items I feel sure enough to test.

Once I have a company that meets these personal requirements of mine I will place an order for at least 3 but up to 5 of the items I am interested in and then select a few other items from the line (that preferably are not for sale on Amazon yet) and add them to the order in a quantity of 2-3 until I hit the initial order requirement. Then once I see how things sell I can make a more informed order the next time increasing my order amount for the winners, leaving out the losers, and always adding in at least one new item to test as I grow the line in my inventory.

I know what you are thinking now: that is all well and good but how the heck do I find the items to sell in the first place? I'm glad you asked!

# Finding items to wholesale

There are many ways to go around finding items that would make good wholesale candidates. In this section we are going to discuss some of the best and along the way I'll share with you how I have used these methods to find the ones that have proven the most successful for me.

## Your own inventory

What better place to start than with items you have already sold? Go through your sales and see what has sold for a good ROI. These can be items you picked up at thrift stores and have sold multiple times or they could be items you have found through retail arbitrage. If you see a pattern of sales emerge on a particular product it is a good candidate to look into wholesale for. For me, this was my eureka moment and led me into the world of wholesale through that mosquito soap I found at the Goodwill. I'd like to think I still would have found my way to wholesale by now but I'm honestly not sure. The ease of order along with the confidence in the product because of the prior sales gave me the confidence I so desperately needed to take that step. Hopefully it will do the same for you if you are wavering at this point and scared to test the waters!

## Friends

Your friends and family can be a valuable resource. There are new products hitting the market and a great way to find the best new ones (that hopefully aren't being sold on Amazon yet or if they are aren't being sold FBA) is to ask around. What are they using? What do they love? What couldn't they live without? Take note and take a look to see if the items are on Amazon.

The second product line I successfully sold came about because of friends. A dear friend of mine holds a "Favorite things" party every year at her house. If you have never been to one before, a Favorite Things Party is a fun gathering where each guest brings several of their favorite item (usually within a set price range). At the party each guest takes turns getting up, telling about their favorite item and why it is their favorite, and then drawing names from a hat to each receive an item. Then the next person goes, and so on, until everyone has had a turn to gush over their item and each guest has some new, highly recommended goodies to try at home.

At this particular party, a guest stood up and presented a fabulous, all natural item that helps to heal chapped hands. I was one of the lucky recipients and still use the product to this day. After my success with the soap I started to rack my brain about what company to contact next and this product was the easy answer. I reached out to the company that produced the product and quickly got signed up. The company is fairly small and the owner handles the orders himself. He had a low minimum and to my surprise a lot more to offer than just the product I had been introduced to. I placed and order for about 6 items in the line and all but one of them has been a winner. 4 of them are big winners that I sell pretty regularly. I pay half retail (about $6-10) and sell for $35 each. I've placed at least 5 new orders with him since the summer and have added a few new items since that initial order that are also doing well.

## Google

Once again Google is your friend. Especially after you have established a niche. There are so many products out there and if you can narrow the field and concentrate on exploring one category of product at a time it will let you be more focused and not miss out on some great finds.

Once I had these items set up and selling well I started to do a little online research every day. As I said before, thrifting wasn't something I could do daily with the kid's home but hopping online with a cup of coffee while they played out back with the neighborhood kids for an hour was. I decided that because the "natural" beauty and health category was treating me well so far that is what I would focus on. My Google searches tended to be along the lines of "Best new natural products", "natural beauty aids you can't live without", "best unknown natural items", etc. And because of my happening upon a product via that Favorite Things party I also spent a good amount of time looking through other peoples posted parties and seeing if I could find some more leads.

From that I found two more lines that are currently doing well. One of them was a bit leary of having a wholesaler sell on the Amazon platform and hadn't explored that market place before. It took a little time to explain the process, and build the trust, but now they are one of my most successful lines and we have a great working relationship. The other is a product that I sell slowly – maybe two a month- but since I clear $30 per sale after Amazon fees I always re-order and keep at least one in my inventory at all times.

**Personal Use**
Just as friends and family can be a good resource…. so can you! Think about the products you use in your own home. Is there a market for them on Amazon? If so do they offer wholesale?

Check your cabinets. Think about your hobbies. Consider what you yourself have searched for and been frustrated because you were unable to find it on Amazon.

That last point is actually how I found another one of my biggest sellers … all because I couldn't find what I wanted on Amazon. Over the summer I had taken up running by way of the Couch to 5K program. I needed something to keep my long hair out of my face and I wanted it to be cuter than just a simple pony tail (After all, I may have been a sweaty, running mess but I could still look fashionable). So, I turned where I always do: Amazon. I couldn't find what I was looking for which seemed crazy to me because, c'mon…it's Amazon!

Frustrated, I turned to Google, but this time to find something that would work for me and not something to sell. Or so I thought. Search after search kept turning up the same results and I was really excited to order it. But, wait… why wasn't it on Amazon? Why didn't I just sell it myself? I could nab a few for myself at great prices and possibly have a great new product line in a new niche. A quick search on the company website revealed that they were very wholesale friendly and within a couple days I was approved to place an order. I had to create a lot (A LOT) of new listings since there were many different variations of the product that I was selling but it was worth it. I pay $4 each and sell them for almost $20 each. And I've sold hundreds. Every order I add new variations and there are still so many to add it will probably take me the rest of the year to get to them all as I place new orders every month or two.

That homerun led me to a new niche. Running gear. It is a new niche that I am working on growing and currently have two lines launched … both doing well. And it is a hobby I enjoy and one that has new items coming out all of the time so it is fun to research and keep up on the latest trends.

# Taking the next step

Ok, here is the scary part. Making contact. The good news is that although you may have visions of placing scary cold calls as I did, in the vast majority of cases this doesn't happen. Most companies have email contact info on their sites and you can generate a nice form letter for your initial contact and then take it from there when you get a response. I introduce myself, explain that I sell on Amazon, briefly share why I am interested in the niche that they sell in, and ask for their wholesale price sheet and order requirements.

That's it. It really isn't scary at all. Some companies will reply back that they only sell to brick and mortar stores. Some will have, the previously mentioned, crazy high order requirements. Some won't have the pricing that you are looking for (I had one company tell me that I am better off continuing to buy from Walmart because the prices they offer wholesale are higher than the shelf prices at Walmart. True Story). But, plenty will send them right over and be happy to have you on board.

Take the time to look over each wholesale price sheet and if you like what you see place that initial order and see what happens.

Once you officially sign on to buy wholesale from a company some will have you sign a contract promising to adhere to what is called the MAP agreement.

MAP, which stands for Minimum Advertised Price, is an agreement between the company and the retailer stipulating the lowest price an item is allowed to be advertised and sold at.

I can tell you that with my personal business model and profit requirements when I buy wholesale this is NEVER a problem. But, it is definitely something some companies are concerned about. They don't want to sell you an item they retail for $20 at a $10 wholesale price and have you sell it on your site for $15. Basically, they don't want you to hurt their personal retail sales.

I recently had a company I am selling for reach out to me and ask me to send them links to my Amazon listings to ensure that I am adhering to the MAP agreement. It is an item I pay $9 for and sell for $35. They sell it for $17 and that is what the MAP agreement states I must sell it for (at the minimum). I told her that wouldn't be a problem and happily sent her the links. She was shocked to say the least and we chatted about it for a bit.

Another company I sell products for in the running niche contacted me after her to let me know that they noticed I was selling their product for $35 and that they found $25 to be the best price for rapid sales of their product. I reminded them that I had quickly sold out at the $35 and am currently waiting for them to restock their own inventory so I can place a new order of my own and thanked them but let them know that while this price is selling through I am not messing with a good thing.

Of course, the danger in all of this is that these companies could opt to come into the market themselves and cash in on a bigger piece of the profits. It's a real possibility and something I constantly keep an eye on but I believe in total honesty with the companies I deal with and if they do decide to sell their products FBA themselves I will respect that and bow out. There are plenty more companies out there waiting to be discovered!

This actually did happen to be recently in a way but at this time they are filling the orders themselves. It is a product that I buy for $29, retails for $59 on their website, and I sell on Amazon for over $70. When I went to check the listing before placing a new order last month (I had sold out of my stock that week) I noticed a new seller had joined the listing I created. Sure enough it is them and they are selling it for the same $59 price as on their website. But, considering I am still the only FBA seller, even at the higher price I got the two sales that week, not them so I will continue to sell their product as long as it continues to sell and they don't switch to FBA.

Of course, it's not all sunshine and roses and every line I test is not a hit. I have tested about 20 wholesale lines at this point and only 7 of them are ones I still order from regularly and are proven winners. But, still that is 7 lines of products that produce steady, reliable income that supplements the other avenues of my business. There were some I would have bet money on being big winners, ones I was really excited about, and the nothing. Not a single sale. So, it can be a gamble but in the end you only need a handful of winners to get started and if you are careful the duds won't cost you too much.

# Putting it all together

The best businesses are well rounded ones.  Especially for this Mom!  Different seasons bring different demands on my time and different focuses on my business.  But, putting together thrifting, retail arbitrage, and wholesale gives me a business that is strong in multiple areas and can weather any storm.

And growing my business in steps, based on my own risk assessment of each, has allowed me to learn along the way and test the waters in one area before adding on the next.

So, what's next?  Well, now that I have expanded into the major areas of the Amazon seller world the only thing left is a website that features my wholesale lines but is done through Amazon so it is all integrated still with their FBA program.

I envision a natural health and beauty type site that features my natural products, my running gear, and anything related that I may explore in the future.  But, for now I have enough on my plate that this is not on my immediate to do list and honestly I do have concerns that people finding me from a platform that does not say Amazon at the top may not as readily pay the same prices I currently am able to sell at.

It is definitely something to think more about but for now I am content thrifting and expanding into new wholesale contracts.

Now you know where I am… what is your next step?  Whatever it is, remember the sky is the limit, you just have to have the courage to reach for it!

First, I want to sincerely thank you for purchasing my book. I know there are a lot of options out there and I'm honored that you decided to come along on this ride with me!

I hope I have been able to shine some light into the world of retail arbitrage and wholesale and that I have given you the tools to take your own business to the next level. If you have enjoyed this book and found it helpful please let me know by reviewing it on Amazon. This helps me write other books and help explain other aspects of business here on Amazon just waiting for you!

If you enjoyed this guide please check out my other books:
**Amazon Mom: One Woman's Journey from Mom to Successful Online Entrepreneur** which can be found here: **http://tinyurl.com/mfl86gz** . It's no secret that finding the perfect work/home balance is a struggle for many people. Read the story of one woman who did just that! Stacy takes you along on her journey from becoming a new Mom to learning and running a successful Amazon business all from the comfort of her own home. This quick read, jam packed with inspiration and information, is destined to get you started on your own journey to a financial freedom. Don't wait another day!

**Amazon Mom - Gettin' Thrifty With It!: How to Turn Thrift Store Finds into Full Time Income** which can be found here: http://www.amazon.com/dp/B00MEVYADG/ref=rdr_kindle_ext_tmb . The original Amazon Mom, Stacy, is back with her second book! In her first book, Stacy shared her story and some tips of the trade. This time she helps get you started on your own journey by using low risk and easy to implement methods. Join Stacy as she explains how to use thrift store finds to help stock your Amazon inventory! You will learn where to look, what to look for, and what to leave on the shelf.

Stacy dishes on a variety of topics: you will learn which items sell best, what to watch out for while shopping, how to bring the kids along on your shopping trips without losing your mind, how to schedule your trips, and much more. You will even come along on a sample thrift store trip and see Stacy's personal methods first hand. This short read is sure to arm you with the information and inspiration you need and have you ready to hit the stores yourself in no time!

Questions? Want to chat? Success story to share?
I would love to hear from you!
You can contact me at:
Email: StacyMcCaff@gmail.com
Twitter: https://twitter.com/StacyMcCaff
Facebook: www.facebook.com/amazonmomstacy
My blog: www.amazonmomblog.com

www.ingramcontent.com/pod-product-compliance
Lightning Source LLC
Chambersburg PA
CBHW082258220526
45469CB00009B/3066